Cinderella

Illustrated by Val Biro

Award Publications Limited

Once upon a time there was a girl called Cinderella.

She lived with her stepmother and stepsisters, who made her their servant.

When an invitation arrived to a ball at the palace, Cinderella was so excited!

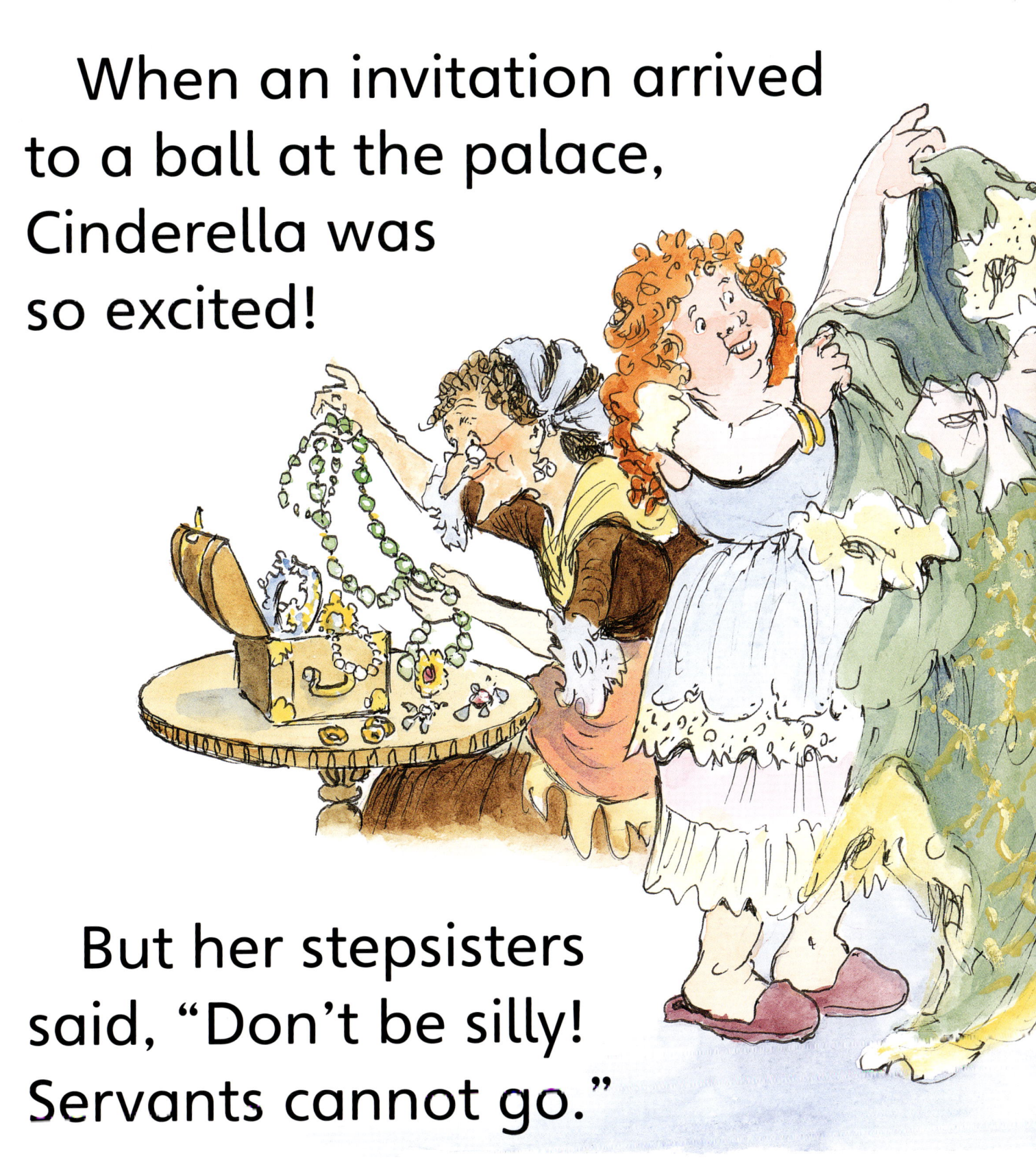

But her stepsisters said, "Don't be silly! Servants cannot go."

When her stepmother and stepsisters left for the ball, Cinderella sat alone by the fire and cried.

Suddenly a fairy appeared. "I'm your Fairy Godmother," she said. "You shall go to the ball."

Cinderella's Fairy Godmother asked her to fetch a pumpkin.

And with a swish of her wand...

...she turned it into a golden carriage!

Cinderella then caught a rat. With another wave of the wand, her Fairy Godmother turned it into a grand horse.

Then she turned some lizards into footmen and a driver.

"There's just one more thing…" said the Fairy Godmother.

With a final swish of the wand, Cinderella's rags turned into a beautiful gown. She looked just like a real princess.

"Remember..." said the Fairy Godmother,

"...on the last stroke of midnight the magic will end."

At the palace, all the guests admired Cinderella. No one recognised her, not even her stepsisters and stepmother.

The prince danced with Cinderella all night. Everyone wanted to know who the beautiful stranger was.

But when the palace clock chimed midnight, Cinderella fled from the ball.

In her hurry to leave, Cinderella dropped one of her glass slippers. The prince told his footmen to find the lady whose foot fit the delicate shoe.

All the women in the town wanted to try it on.

The stepsisters' feet were too big. "Is there anyone else here?" the footmen asked.

"Only our servant, Cinderella," replied the stepsisters.

Cinderella was called. The glass slipper was a perfect fit!

And to everyone's surprise,
she produced the matching shoe.

Her Fairy Godmother appeared and waved her wand. Cinderella was transformed once again.

The stepsisters asked Cinderella to forgive them for treating her so cruelly.

The prince was overjoyed to be reunited with Cinderella, and they were married the next day. The stepsisters married the footmen too, and they all lived happily ever after.